YOUR KNOWLEDGE HAS VALUE

- We will publish your bachelor's and master's thesis, essays and papers

- Your own eBook and book - sold worldwide in all relevant shops

- Earn money with each sale

Upload your text at www.GRIN.com
and publish for free

Bibliographic information published by the German National Library:

The German National Library lists this publication in the National Bibliography; detailed bibliographic data are available on the Internet at http://dnb.dnb.de .

Imprint:

Copyright © 2009 GRIN Verlag, Open Publishing GmbH
Print and binding: Books on Demand GmbH, Norderstedt Germany
ISBN: 9783640600205

This book at GRIN:

http://www.grin.com/en/e-book/148160/murder-on-behalf-of-science

Melanie Buchmayr

Murder on behalf of science?

Stem cell research and ethics

GRIN Publishing

GRIN - Your knowledge has value

Since its foundation in 1998, GRIN has specialized in publishing academic texts by students, college teachers and other academics as e-book and printed book. The website www.grin.com is an ideal platform for presenting term papers, final papers, scientific essays, dissertations and specialist books.

Visit us on the internet:

http://www.grin.com/

http://www.facebook.com/grincom

http://www.twitter.com/grin_com

JOHANNES KEPLER
UNIVERSITÄT LINZ
Netzwerk für Forschung, Lehre und Praxis

Conference paper

Text Production II: Academic and Professional Writing

at the institute for Fachsprachen

547.77E SS 2009

Buchmayr Melanie

Murder on behalf of science?

Stem cell research and ethics.

Deadline: June 10th, 2009

Abstract

(Embryonic) stem cell research is still highly controversial even if confronted with the vast of chances this new technology might bring to mankind. People with strong ethnic and/or religious beliefs struggle with the idea of having the embryos "killed" in order to produce the valuable stem cells.

This paper will focus on the conflict of ethnical beliefs versus scientific progress. It will cover the basic differences between adult stem cell research and embryonic stem cell research, what the arguments of both sides are and how this conflict is dealt with in the EU.   (93 words)

Keywords: Stem cell research, ethics, controversy, religion, legislation

1. Introduction

"Thou shalt not kill" is probably the most important commandment of Christianity. Therefore, controversy with embryonic stem cell research seems to be bound to occur. For various reasons, the issue of stem cell research is a very dramatic topic to many people. One needs to ask him- or herself if a cluster of cells should be considered as life equal to a born child's life or if mankind is actually facing the most progressive chance in science.

The most comprehensible argument against stem cell research would be the usage and, therefore, destruction of healthy, viable embryonic cells. The possibility to use cells provided by adults is often mentioned by pro-life activists as the far better solution. The reason behind this might be the religious background of many pro-life activists, which is grounded in their belief that no one but God can give and take life. In 2008, the United States Conference of Catholic Bishops released a statement on this matter: "[...] Harvesting these 'embryonic stem cells' involves the deliberate killing of innocent human beings, a gravely immoral act. Yet some try to justify it by appealing to a hoped-for future benefit to others" (Malloy, 2008, p. 2). Their choice of word clearly shows their attitude.

Up to now, people suffering from incurable, terminal diseases might understand this point of view as provocation, irrationalism and actually self-contradicting as it condemns them to death. The scientific side is aware of the ethical discussion and states that human dignity needs to be respected but also "considers it important to take into account, based on a precautionary approach, the potential long-term consequences of stem cell research and use for individuals and the society" (McLaren, Hermerén, 2000, p. 15).

Outcome is a highly controversial field of research. This paper concentrates on exploring how patients, scientists, the Church and the legislation of the USA and the EU deal with this issue.

2. Embryonic stem cell research – adult stem cell research

Stem cells are cells that can divide to produce either cells like themselves (self-renewal) or cells of one or several specific differentiated types. Stem cells are not yet fully differentiated and therefore can reconstitute one or several types of tissues (McLaren & Hermerén, 2000, p. 3).

General somatic cells usually hold a very specific purpose within an animal's or the human's body. In opposition to that the body also produces stem cells. Those cells are the most important set of cells as they are unique and not specialized to certain functions: These cells are able to grow into some or even all of the more than 200 different body cell types. Thus, stem cells have a particular role in repairing organs and body tissues throughout life and are – against common belief – not only found in embryos. Early-stage embryos have a far greater variety in stem cells though. Therefore, stem cells retrieved from embryos are more compatible to different types of body cells and are more likely to repair damages than adult stem cells (Johnson & Williams, 2007, p. 3). Given this information it is necessary to define how stem cells, i.e. both embryonic and adult stem cells, are retrieved and how the cells may be applied within different therapies.

2.1.   Definitions & differences

There are different methods of how to obtain embryonic stem cells. It is possible to derive stem cells from in-vitro-fertilisation (IVF) embryos or from foetal tissue. This is one of the most controversial points as taking the cells from very early-stage embryos destroys them. Most abortion opponents also adjudge this science as cruel and unethical. Different methods have been developed to produce embryonic stem cells; the IVF-method developed by the University of Wisconsin is the most common today. The embryos used were originally created for the treatment of infertility. The parents may choose to dispose of the excess embryos, make them available for research causes, or have another couple adopt an embryo (Johnson & Williams, 2007, pp. 5-6).

Cloning (SCNT = somatic cell nuclear transfer) also enables embryonic stem cell production. To retrieve stem cells the SCNT-created cell needs to age for a few days. SCNT derived stem cells would be identical to the originally provided cells from the patient, and therefore, are the best choice for therapy purposes as they prevent tissue rejection (Johnson & Williams, 2007, pp. 6-7).

The third variation of obtaining stem cells is from adult organisms. In 2007, cells comparable to embryonic stem cells were found in amniotic fluid. Experts, however, advised not to consider this a full replacement for embryonic stem cells. Various other publications mentioned retrieving adult stem cells from different sources, such as bone marrow and the umbilical cord (Johnson & Williams, 2007, pp. 8-9).

3. Pros & cons

Last century's discovery of how to isolate and culture human embryonic cells is being described as one of the most significant breakthroughs in biomedicine. The culturing of human embryonic stem cells holds great potential for both developments of new forms of medicine as well as ethical discussions. It may seem ironic that this amazing discovery should bring up some of the most intractable questions about the value of life itself. Neither is a justified and definite response to such a question obvious, nor is it immediately apparent. One should engage with these questions, however, as they are probably unsurpassed in their depth, complexity and importance (Rickard, 2002, p. 7).

3.1.   The basic ethical problem

Rickard (2002, p.8) explains this basic problem well in his report for the Australian government: The possibility of embryonic stem cell research presents mankind with a moral problem. Two fundamental moral principles seem to be affected: One principle enjoins the prevention or alleviation of suffering, and the other enjoins us to respect the value of human life.

However, it is mentioned that producing human embryonic stem cells violates the second principle due to the destruction of human life with value (e.g. human embryos). Apparently, it is not possible to respect both principles simultaneously. So this leads to the question which one of the principles holds the priority of rank in this controversy. As Rickard (2002, p.8) mentions, the questions to be answered are firstly if people should give more weight to the first, and permit destructive embryonic stem cell research because of its remarkable potential benefits, or if the second should be weighted stronger, and prohibit destructive embryonic research because it violates respect for the value of the embryo as the beginning of a possible human life.

It might sound insensitive but the answer lies within making a decision about how the positive value of destructive embryo research is to be weighted, from a moral point of view, in comparison to the negative value of destroying embryos. The most important outcome is probably not solving the problem once and for all, but rather getting a clear idea of what moral weight each side of the equation has. Therefore, this includes firstly, developing a clear image of what the real value and benefits of embryonic research are, and secondly, elucidating the value of embryos themselves, and what, if anything, may be wrong with destroying them (Rickard, 2002, p. 9).

3.2.   The Value of the Embryo

As explained before, arguments about the rightness or wrongness of destroying embryos are based on one's view about the moral status of the embryo. It seems relatively uncontroversial to describe embryos as human life. On the other hand, though, it is rather controversial to describe embryos as persons, human beings, or potential persons, etc. Needless to say those descriptions are morally charged. There are different implications, though; whether they are reasonable will depend on the nature and plausibility of the particular arguments that accompany each view on the moral status of the embryo. Primarily, assumptions are that embryos have the status of either persons, potential persons, 'divine creations', subjects of moral 'harm', the beginnings of human life (with intrinsic value), or organic material with no more moral standing than other body parts (Rickman, 2007, p.13).

Without clear legislation and governmental definition of the value of embryos, research will never be possible with clear conscience (see chapter 4).

3.3. The Catholic Church

Malloy (2008) quotes Pope Benedict XVI as of January 2008 that the Catholic Church "appreciates and encourages the progress of the biomedical sciences which open up unprecedented therapeutic prospects". The Church wants to point out that life is the first and most basic gift from an infinitely loving God and, therefore, deserves utmost respect and protection. It condemns 'researchers, ethicists, and policy makers' who claim that science may directly kill innocent embryonic human beings as if they were mere objects of research – and even that taxpayers are accomplices in such killing through use of public funds.

The Church claims that no commitment to a hoped-for 'greater good' can diminish the wrong of directly taking innocent human lives here and now. Malloy (2008) argues that the same ethic that justifies taking lives to help the patient with Parkinson's or Alzheimer's disease today can be used to sacrifice that very patient tomorrow, if his or her survival is viewed as disadvantaging other human beings considered more deserving or productive.

Furthermore, Malloy stresses that a human embryo, from conception onward, is as much a living member of the human species as anybody. He even proceeds to mention that it is a biological fact that a new living organism has the full complement of human genes and is actively expressing those genes to live and develop in a way that is unique to human beings, setting the essential foundation for further development. Although he admits that this cluster of cells is "dependent in many ways", Malloy goes on to say embryos are complete and distinct members of the species Homo sapiens and that everyone matters to God, no matter how weak or small, and therefore is of concern to the Church (Malloy, 2008, pp.6-8).

Malloy's explanations even reach the point where he – in the name of the Church – advices scientists to only use adult tissue as adult stem cells and umbilical cord blood "are now known to be much more versatile than once thought" (Malloy, 2008, p.8). Trying to make the Church seem to be approving of scientific progression, he emphasises that there is no moral objection to research and therapy of this kind, when it involves no harm to human beings at any stage of development: "We must pursue progress in ethically responsible ways that respect the dignity of each human being. Only this will produce cures and treatments that everyone can live with" (Malloy, 2008, pp.8-10).

4. Legislation

4.1. EU

The following graphic shows the complicated legislation concerning stem cell research all over the world. As the reader can see, there are many differences in regulations, especially in Europe.

Figure 1: Global situation concerning stem cell research in September 2008

Source: StemGen (2008): Stem Cell World Map. URL: http://www.stemgen.org/mapworld.cfm (download: April 30th, 2009)

According to a report of the European Group on Ethics in Science and new technologies to the European Commission (McLaren, Hermerén, 2000, p. 10), Ireland is the only country of the EU whose Constitution affirms the right to life of the 'unborn' and that this right is equal to that of the mother. In some Member States, no legislation on embryo research exists at all, such as in Luxemburg or Slovakia for example. Interestingly though, this report still states Italy as not having any legislation on this matter but as the reader can see from the graphic, Italy now has similarly strict regulations as Austria or Germany. Belgium, Spain, Sweden and the UK are the only nations within the EU to authorise research under specified conditions.

Using this graph, a global overview has been given. It is necessary, though, to point out that it is outdated already: US-President Barack Obama signed the new US-stem cell research policy in March 2009. In his speech, Obama also responded to the scepticism towards stem cell research. He emphasised the fact that new potential will not reveal itself on its own, resp. that medical miracles do not happen simply by accident. Furthermore, he talked about the opportunities the country missed during former governmental periods:

> "[...] in recent years, when it comes to stem cell research, rather than furthering discovery, our government has forced what I believe is a false choice between sound science and moral values. In this case, I believe the two are not inconsistent. As a person of faith, I believe we are called to care for each other and work to ease human suffering. I believe we have been given the capacity and will to pursue this research – and the humanity and conscience to do so responsibly. It is a difficult and delicate balance. Many thoughtful and decent people are conflicted about, or strongly oppose, this research. I understand their concerns, and we must respect their point of view" (The White House press release, 2009).

5. Conclusion

Exploring both sides of an argument without being prejudiced is not an easy task. This article focused on researching from a rational, less emotional point of view.

As the reader learned, during the Bush Administration in the USA ethical issues were prioritised to health issues although several organisations such as the National Aca-demics favoured "more embryonic stem cell research than the Bush policy allowed"

(Johnson & Williams, 2004, p. 22). The new Obama Administration, however, signed the new stem cell research policy on March 9th, 2009. President Obama stated in his speech that this "[...] will bring the change that so many scientists and researchers; doctors and innovators; patients and loved ones have hoped for, and fought for, these past eight years [...]" (The White House press release, 2009), laying the foundation for another massive and needed change in policy. Austria, in comparison, is far behind in adapting legislation in this field; and a change of thinking is not to be expecting soon.

The Catholic Church, both in the USA and the EU, condemns the use of embryonic cells because of the religious background of the Ten Commandments but also due to serious doubts regarding the ethics of experimenting on human cells.

Putting aside those doubts and an almost inflated discussion about ethics, all that is left is people suffering, on the one hand, and a chance to cure them, on the other hand. Waiting for a higher being's or its "representatives'" blessing is a waste of valuable time as the paper shows. Facing more and more seemingly incurable diseases, mankind should face its responsibility and take action now.

Words: ~2,400

Johnson, Judith A. & Williams, Erin (2007): Stem Cell Research: Federal Research
    Funding and Oversight. CRS Report for Congress, URL:
    http://ncseonline.org/NLE/CRSreports/07March/RL33540.pdf (download: March
    22nd, 2009)

Malloy, David (2008): A Statement of the United States Conference of Catholic Bish-
    ops, URL: http://www.usccb.org/prolife/issues/bioethic/bishopsESCRstmt.pdf
    (download: March 22nd, 2009)

McLaren, Anne & Hermerén, Göran (2000): Opinion of the European Group on Ethics
    in Science and new technologies to the European Commission. Ethnical Aspects
    of Stem Cell Research and use,
    URL: http://ec.europa.eu/european_group_ethics/docs/avis15_en.pdf
    (download: March 22nd, 2009)

Rickard, Maurice Dr, Department of the Parliamentary Library of Australia (2002):
    Key Ethical Issues in Embryonic Stem Cell Research,
    URL: http://www.aph.gov.au/library/pubs/CIB/2002-03/03cib05.pdf (download:
    March 22nd, 2009)

StemGen (2008): Stem Cell World Map. Global situation concerning stem cell re-
    search in September 2008, URL: http://www.stemgen.org/mapworld.cfm
    (download: April 30th, 2009)

The White House Office of Press Secretary (2009): "Signing of Stem Cell Executive
    Order and Scientific Integrity Presidential",
    URL: http://www.whitehouse.gov/the_press_office/Remarks-of-the-President-As-
    Prepared-for-Delivery-Signing-of-Stem-Cell-Executive-Order-and-Scientific-
    Integrity-Presidential-Memorandum/ (download: March 22nd, 2009)

YOUR KNOWLEDGE HAS VALUE

- We will publish your bachelor's and master's thesis, essays and papers

- Your own eBook and book - sold worldwide in all relevant shops

- Earn money with each sale

Upload your text at www.GRIN.com and publish for free